Life in a Wetland

Doris Dumrauf

Paperback ISBN: 978-0-9976767-2-3
Hardback ISBN: 978-0-9976767-4-7

Library of Congress Control Number: 2020909432

Produced by: Saloff Enterprises
Cover by: Mark Saloff Designs
Author Photo by: Nicole MC Photography

When I am not photographing birds and other wildlife in my back yard, I am often drawn to water. One of my greatest pleasures is a hike through a local marsh or state park because I am fascinated by the abundance of wildlife and plants that depend on wetlands for their survival.

The wildlife depicted in this book are just a small sampling of the many species that call North American wetlands home.

This book complements my other books, "Create Your Own Backyard Wildlife Habitat" and "Common Backyard Birds."

I hope it will inspire you to explore wetlands in your neighborhood and beyond.

Happy birding!

Doris Dumrauf
Spring 2020

Great Blue Heron

As the largest heron in North America, I may look clumsy and slow but don't be fooled. While I often stand still or stalk my prey with slow steps, I grab it with my long bill at lightning speed. I live alone most of the year except during breeding season, when I nest in large tree colonies.

Mallard

I am the ancestor of most domestic ducks. As a dabbling duck, I eat by tipping my head down into the water. In parks, I am tame and will even accept handouts from humans, but please don't feed me bread or other processed foods. Peas, corn, rice, or chopped greens are much better for me.

Anhinga

My nickname is "snake bird" because you can only see my head and neck above water when I am swimming in lakes and ponds. I eat mostly fish, which I spear with my impressive bill. After a swim, I spread out my wings and lift my head high to dry.

American Bullfrog

Walk by any pond, lake, or marsh and you may hear me roaring like a bull. My favorite food: anything that fits into my big mouth, even fish, mice, birds, and small snakes. I hunt at night and will jump up to six feet to catch my dinner!

Wood Duck

I am one of the most handsome ducks if I may say so myself. Look for me in wooded swamps, marshes, or streams. I nest in tree holes or nest boxes near water. Just a day after my eggs hatch, my downy ducklings jump up to 50 feet down from the tree, land unhurt on the ground, and follow their mother straight to the water.

Tricolored Heron

I am a medium-sized heron with a big personality. Watch me while I am hunting for food and you will think I am performing in a solo show. I flap my wings and run until I stop in my tracks to catch a meal of small fish.

Snowy Egret

My black bill and yellow feet set me apart from my larger relative, the great egret. I use those feet to stir up my prey of small aquatic animals. You will find me in coastal regions most of the year, but during breeding season my range is much larger. My preferred habitat is mud flats, beaches, and marshes.

Canada Goose

My ability to digest grass makes me a familiar sight in grain fields, parks, and lawns all over North America. I am commonly seen in flocks and fly in a V-formation. This form of flying helps us fly faster: each one of us flies a bit above the bird in front of us, which reduces wind resistance.

I am a common sight in freshwater habitats all over North America. After sleeping at the bottom of a lake or stream at night, I spend summer days catching sunrays on a log or rock with my friends. I like it warm because I am cold blooded. After my body is warmed up, I hunt for vegetation, insects, and aquatic life.

Great Egret

Bird watchers are dazzled by my beauty when they spot me in wetlands. I often stand still while hunting before I stab a fish with my long yellow bill.

During breeding season, I grow long plumes (feathers) on my back to impress the females. I nest in tree colonies high above the ground.

Great Egret

Little Blue Heron

As an adult, I am not very colorful but as a youth I was bright white. That way I could blend in among snowy egrets to catch more food. Slow and steady is my motto when I am hunting for fish in shallow water. Look closely at water's edge or nearby vegetation and you might see me.

White Ibis

It is hard to overlook me because I am almost entirely white with red-orange legs and bill. I use my large bill to feel through the mud for my next catch. As a social bird, you'll likely see me in large flocks in coastal wetlands of the Southeast.

Twelve-Spotted Skimmer

When I am not darting through the air, you may see me resting on a perch near water. The facets in my eyes give me almost 360-degree vision. As a dragonfly, I am one of the world's fastest insects. Mosquitoes and other small insects are no match for me. Even as an aquatic nymph, I was feasting on mosquito larvae.

Great Spangled Fritillary

I get my name from the checkerboard pattern on my wings and am a common sight throughout much of the eastern United States. While I lay my eggs only on violets, I am not a picky eater as an adult. I can't resist drinking nectar from milkweeds, but I also visit many other plants all summer long.

Double-Crested Cormorant

I may look like just another dark bird to you, but up close my eyes dazzle like a precious stone. Because my feet are webbed, I can chase my prey of fish under water. After a swim, I spread my soaked wings to dry them in the sun.

Osprey

I am also known as a fish hawk because I mostly eat live fish. That's why your best chance of seeing me is near a river, lake, or marsh. When I'm hungry, I hunt with outstretched feet to snatch fish with barbed pads like hooks under my toes. Pretty awesome, isn't it?

Red-Winged Blackbird

I am a familiar sight in North American marshes and my song is one of a kind: Conk-la-ree! During breeding season, I sing my heart out from high perches while spreading out my colorful wings. That should keep any intruders out of my territory. My mate doesn't look much like me, and some people are surprised to learn we are the same species.

I hunt for insects as I fly over wetlands and fields. While I prefer to nest in tree cavities, I will gladly accept a clean nest box. When I am not breeding, I am very sociable and join huge flocks of my friends at roost sites.

Green Heron

If you look closely at the edges and vegetation of shallow water, you might see me, my eyes cast downward to the water. My long beak is fearsome by itself, but I also use tools—bread, insects, and feathers—as bait to lure fish closer. That's pretty smart, don't you think?

American White Pelican

Despite my large size (bigger than a Canada goose) I soar through the skies with calm, steady wing beats. On the water, I scoop up fish with my massive orange bill and swallow it whole. My appetite is huge: I eat more than four pounds of fish per day! I spend summers at inland lakes and winters near coastlines.

American Alligator

Find me in freshwater habitats in the southeastern United States, but don't get too close. I seem to walk slowly on land, but I move at high speed to catch my prey. At a length of eleven to fifteen feet I am an apex predator. That means I am at the very top of the food chain.

About Wetlands:

North American wetlands consist of many different habitats: rivers, lakes, marshes, swamps, bogs, lake shores, vernal pools, and prairie potholes. They all have one feature in common: they are covered by water for all or part of the year. As such, they are a haven for birds, insects, amphibians, and plants. One third of North American bird species rely on wetlands as breeding and feeding sites.

Florida's Everglades, the largest marsh system in the United States, is saturated by a slow-moving river that originates in Lake Okeechobee. The Everglades provide habitat for thousands of species of birds, fish, mammals, reptiles, and insects.

Wetlands serve as important buffers because they slow the progress of hurricanes and help prevent flooding by absorbing stormwater runoff. They also filter toxins, sediments, and nutrients from surface waters, thereby improving our air and water quality.

Take time to visit a wetland near you and look at the animals and plants that call wetlands home!

About the Author

Doris Dumrauf is an award-winning author, nature photographer, and public speaker. She has published numerous photo features in magazines and newspapers.

She collected the images in this book during travels to Ohio, southern Florida, and near her home. Doris lives in western Pennsylvania with her husband, two indoor cats, and a back yard full of birds and other wildlife.

Visit Doris at:
DorisDumrauf.com
DorisDumraufAuthor.com
Instagram: dumraufdoris

Nonfiction books:
Create Your Own Backyard Wildlife Habitat
Common Backyard Birds

Awards:
First Place Best Photography 2019 Purple Dragonfly Book Awards
Silver/Second Place 2019 Feathered Quill Book Awards Program in the Children's Early Readers (6-8) category

CPSIA information can be obtained
at www.ICGtesting.com
Printed in the USA
LVIC060213180920
666450LV00001B/2
* 9 7 8 0 9 9 7 6 7 6 7 2 3 *